just BE here

just **BE** here

The Guide

to

Musicking Mindfulness

Simon Cole

mindful
writing

Other books by the same author:

Essentials for Living in a Troubled World
    (Amazon 2020)

Pathways : humanity's search for its soul
    (2nd edition, Amazon 2019)

Stillness in Mind : a companion to mindfulness,
meditation and living
    (Changemakers Books, 2014)

Being Still, Being Now : a companion to
mindfulness
    (Amazon, 2013)

Contents

*In memory of my father
who introduced me to music*

INTRO

no previous musical experience required

L et me be clear from the start:

1. 'Musicking' is only a little to do with music as we
. usually think of it

2. You are reading about an alternative approach to
learning and practising the technique of
mindfulness

3. It is about more than mindfulness, it is about
Flow

You should not be put off by this book being thinner,
more readable (hopefully), and (generally) simpler
sounding, than most offerings on this subject. Because
the essential part of mindfulness *is* simple, so simple in
fact that we knew it and practised it right back when we
relied on finding berries and spearing wild animals for
food... and then lost it when we started getting clever
(young children and animals still have it) -

it's no more than this:

JUST BE HERE

Simple doesn't always mean easy. Each of those words begs a few questions, but for now let them sit in your mind as a seed ready to germinate. They are like the tonic key of our melody.

If you're worried about the 'musicking' bit and think it might be a gimmick, don't be. I'm not the first person to put a 'k' on music to indicate the process of making and exchanging musical experiences, but I give it a more specialised use because I bring in a much more extended idea of what the exchanges can be - more of that later.

Another thing - 'Mindfulness' is not what we are really trying to master here. Long long ago I found that 'Mindfulness', as people generally wrote about it and taught it, had too static a feel if you were into music. Music flows - we talk about passages and phrases and movements. And actually, so does living, flow that is. Life is analogue, not digital - not a series of individual camera shots which each capture a slice of time. When you 'walk' through your day in your mind, does it feel like you cut from one scene to the next? Even if certain highlight events stand out, there was always the same 'you' joining up the scenes.

So your life doesn't jump from scene to scene, because living flows like music flows and most of us have a sense that, if we can just keep the flow going fairly smoothly, we will be alright.

As a therapist, what I have observed over the years is that distress results when the flow stops, and more and more I have looked for *how* an individual's flow has been disturbed, rather than *what* are the symptoms and where is the remedy. Saying that "distress results when the flow stops" is really no different from that well-known saying of the Buddha that "all suffering comes from holding on". Most often *we* stop the flow, by allowing something to get stuck. It has to be down to us: in the end we cannot abdicate our duty to look after our own life.

And so, not so much just Mindfulness, really this book is about the Flow... in these three aspects:

- **Musicking** - the 'k' is there because it *may* be, but it doesn't *have* to be, about making music in the way we conventionally think of it in any of our various cultures

- **Dialoguing** - in all the ways we exchange between each other - not just talking but also in how we lean into our exchanges with others in ways which reveal our genuineness, honesty, graciousness, regard

- **Levelling** - the understanding of how we distort our idea of what our world is really like, and shoot ourselves in the foot in the process

There is no clear boundary between any of these, but the one which in a sense is the key and the 'motor' for keeping the wheel steadily turning is the last one. None, though, is just itself and, like a good solo player will draw on the contribution of each person in the band for their improvisation, so each component complements and completes the other two in our quest to live with more balance and contentment.

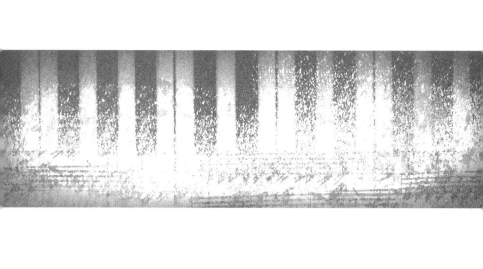

THE 8-BAR BLUES

the Blues of this modern life

L et me play you a piece of a life, not my life particularly, though in parts there will be likenesses, not your life particularly, though in parts there will be likenesses there too, just a life set somewhere sometime...

'First off, She couldn't move. Waking up, or woken up, in the middle of a dream - why do dreams never finish? - and now a kind of weighed-down struggling to come round, with a gnawing edge of something hanging and knowing She had not done good and, wherever it was the dream had deposited Her, She'd not come off well. The usual.

And then, He had edged Her over on her side and now, flat out on his back, spreadeagled arms and legs akimbo, He must have pushed Her into the narrowest strip She could hold onto without falling on the floor. Typical.

She rolled out, staggered to her feet, did the necessary, found herself in the kitchen without knowing what had happened in between... coffee, yoghurt, toast... slowly her brain starting to give her sentences, sort of, still something gnawing, but now, instead of the acute prickling sense of having failed, which seemed to be tinged with guilt, it was a dreariness which seemed to surround Her like a fog and take away the interest or even image of anything outside her immediate periphery.

He woke suddenly like someone had switched on his current and robot-like leapt into life, meticulously with great alacrity attended to his toilet - shaving? yes, today, smart casual, the shirt ironed last night and a jacket, checked the necessaries were in the right pockets - sailed down to the kitchen, ok for time? yes, carefully laid his breakfast, coffee ground (the Ethiopian this time) for a lengthened espresso, and He'd planned Greek yoghurt for this morning. Then got up, cleared up, washed up - putting the mugs and dishes away - again this flash He sometimes had, quite odd, his parents' kitchen cupboard, and its monotonous neatness - then out, just in time for the bus.

She'd already left. They didn't meet, even accidentally.

The clatter on the metro seemed especially jarring, or was it just her hangover state (which actually wasn't a hangover, this was how it often was these days), but this morning it was so strident, the noise and the clamour that She got off early and walked the rest. And now, sitting down - not having to fight for a space was a relief - She could just wait until her head lightened.

12

But it felt like it would take a while this morning. Head in hands, somebody noticed, but She waved them away. Now alone for a few minutes - She'd made it, as She always did, along the way remembering that She'd never even seen him, let alone said 'Hi', and went out to face her public. (Rather grandiose, but that's the way She always said it in her head.) The 'public' all had issues and She had sympathy of course, but She had issues too, just not the same ones, and there was no-one to have sympathy with Her. There never had been. So probably She was in the wrong job. Of course it would be easier if some of the 'clients' would show a bit of gratitude for what She did for them, heaven knows, She would, if She got the same help with her problems, but She couldn't remember when that had happened. Not ever.

The office had over-booked Him this morning. Of course his admin was more difficult because He had two centres, but it could be done, and here they seemed to forget that He had to have 5 minutes between each patient, not as if He didn't keep to his part, never overran, He needed to clear his head, arrange his room again then sit still and quiet for 2 minutes. He could feel the tenseness coming - in his neck, one shoulder stiff and slightly raised - and He hadn't even started yet. How was He going to get through? No, don't even ask the question, there's no answer, and then He'll feel the panic starting.

Department meeting. She dreaded them. So repetitive, all of them taking their usual positions, all of them bringing in their usual gripes, pushing their usual agendas and they'd all go away again and simply carry on. Because nobody listened. But what was the point of listening because you'd heard it all before? Perhaps this morning She should say something different just for the sake of it. Just to see if anything *could* change. But it wouldn't work. There were a few there who just spouted on and there was no stopping them until they stopped themselves, so they never heard anyone else. And there were others who asked you questions but weren't interested in the answer. No, just sit quiet and try not to be noticed. The usual.

There was something else He couldn't quite work out. He hadn't seen Her at all this morning, which was unusual. Perhaps that had unsteadied Him. But the first person was already coming down the corridor. Got to start. And keep going. Through the morning He felt more and more breathless, even though He wasn't actually out of breath. Psychosomatic. But it felt physical. The office mustn't do this again... must keep to his timings.

They arrived home together from their opposite directions. It didn't often happen and there was no protocol for when it did. She sat down, no, flopped down, to catch up on her phone, He had a shower and if She hadn't been glued to her screen She would have wondered why He always took so long, obsessive her friend called him, though the same friend also remarked approvingly how He *always* seemed so trim - "nicely presented". She didn't notice.

They ate together, though different meals, but shared the wine. Closer later watching a film together on the sofa He noticed how down She was, as if her day had dragged after a bad start and no inspiration and how She now seemed resigned and lifeless. Leaning into Him on the sofa, She felt Him tense, not like taut, but almost as if He was quivering at a cellular level. She knew He took a long time to unwind so She just held him gently and waited. He felt Her closely holding Him, not lifeless now.'

Do you remember the film 'Sliding Doors'? Helen gets fired and rushes to catch a train home, she catches it but gets home to discover her husband in bed with another woman. But then, she might have missed the train, got home later and never found out about her husband's infidelity. The film tracks the alternative lives which would ensue and slews us from one to the other and back as if they were running simultaneously on either slide of a sliding glass door.

Every moment of our every day opens up similar divergent possibilities, the consequences perhaps not so dramatic, though of course we never actually know. But I'm not thinking about the divergence which can result from some chance early departure or late arrival, I have in mind the ways in which we alter the course of events constantly through how we are. All sorts of reasons (excuses) spring to mind - mood, last night's curry, bad hair day, Him (or Her) - that we don't really believe, but that might just let us off the hook for spoiling someone else's day - and then of course there's our past history and attitude which comes up in any situation - yet none of these have any real connection with the individual situations that confront us.

We make the connections ourselves as we encounter whatever and whoever appears in our day. At least a 'we' does, whichever 'we' it might be. I say 'whichever' because without the overlay of all that stuff our head's brought in - from a couple of minutes ago, a couple of hours ago, last year, when we were 6 - it would be a different 'we' and then the ensuing path of life (their's and our's) would be different, like another life the other side of a sliding door.

Whatever we do, it makes a difference.

How we are, makes a difference, and defines our course.

From every point in space and time lead two courses at least, the one masked by all the baggage we have brought, and another seen clearly - unclouded by our illusions and our imaginings.

The metaphor of a sliding door helps to keep in our mind that adopting a 'mindful way of being' is not a change which involves a major decision like moving home or changing job or having a family, it's not that sort of 'big thing'. Except that in other ways it is, because in the end it makes the life that comes from any of those major decisions more satisfying.

So, hold on to the sliding door image - you can see (and soon you'll feel) what's different, and you will be able to slide through to the other side more and more often as you get to appreciate how much better it feels. (Of course Helen in the film isn't completely sure which side is better, until the end that is. But I think you will feel the difference sooner.)

I've mentioned the three aspects of the Flow and we'll look at each for themselves - they'll each have a solo - but the Flow integrates them so that in reality they don't have a completely independent existence - if one is there, they're all there… they're symbiotic really.

I have a definition for **Musicking** which leaves out the word 'music' completely, because it is the "deliberate, non-spoken, expression of feeling or emotion in a way which can shift the feelings or emotions of oneself or another person". So it includes playing music, or singing, or humming, or rap, but it also includes poetry and dancing and making faces, and swirling your arms about and standing on one leg, and waving wistfully as your friend's train pulls away. Musicking is expressing ourselves in an intended or spontaneous way without *meaning* it to make a difference to someone else (though it most often does) and without it making a difference to us *how* it is received by others.

In terms of the musicking which would strike us as 'obviously being music', perhaps my definition is especially useful for us in the West today where the predominant function of music is entertainment. It's not like that in all cultures - in some it's devotional, in some it's medicinal, in some it's a formal part of how a society operates as a group, occasionally it even takes the part of some conversation... if only we didn't so readily extrapolate from our own experience (which is a good caution for mindfulness too)!

Dialoguing seems to be close to Musicking sometimes, but it always has someone else in its sights. We don't generally do Dialoguing with ourselves (though sometimes we find we're talking to ourselves), and the 'dia' implies two, so it assumes we get something back which we take in and which means something to us. There are different versions of dialogue (more about that later), but it sits in the middle of our three aspects of musicking mindfulness here because it is what creates the relationship between us and the outside world.

Levelling is about attitude. It's about those times that we *would* do something for someone if it weren't for something about them (which usually means something about us), and those times when we *would* do something which would make us feel better ourselves except that we never do because we've told ourselves we

17

don't believe in 'that stuff'. It's also about how we don't
hear the words because we're still looking at the hair
style, and we can't even imagine the fond father in the
loud teenage youth. Levelling is the shift we have to
make so that we can see the world as it really is, instead
of how we- *assume, would like, believe, misrepresent,
prejudge, misinterpret, 'need'* -it to be.

In that piece of a life I played, the only (real) Dialoguing
came right at the end. Plenty of non-dialoguing, plenty
of chances for real Dialoguing, but it was not until They
were finally together on the sofa and He had a sense of
how it was for Her - resigned and lifeless - and She for
Him - still vibrating with his tension - that the Levelling
could happen. At that moment for each, the other one
came into view, really into view that is, as another
human being who often like them must submit to what
they feel and sometimes, without a certain kind of help,
will be imprisoned, or maybe not that bad, but still
impeded, until the outside world diverts them with
some escapist unreality.

And there, at the end too, was the Musicking - He, just
noticing and softening (because a sudden empathy will
always relay itself physically); She, leaning in to Him,
holding, waiting.

Now, finally, with the two themes intertwined, the
possibility of Flow.

the 8-bar blues

SOLO 1

set the rhythm, here's the tune

first the beat......

You wouldn't usually give the first solo to the bass player, but here goes anyway.

Music is rhythm... and melody... and timbre (that's the sound of the individual instruments, if you like).

Always music has rhythm. If not, it's noise.

And a life always needs Flow, then it has balance. If not, it's rudderless, adrift on an endless ocean.

You want rhythm? Start by walking! - across the room, down the garden, it doesn't matter. Do it now.

Now do it again, only this time do it differently, just for the sake of it. Slower, faster, hip swing, whatever takes your fancy. See how many ways you can invent to walk those few steps. But also listen, not with your ears, or not mainly with your ears - listen with an internal ear, which really means sensing what the body feels like, when you are doing something. It might need a bit of practice, but not much.

Now the bass player is going to get into a bit of variation. This time change from one walking style to another mid-walk, and then maybe another, all the time listening with your internal ear. And finally decide which one you like the feel of most right now and do a last couple of laps with that, listening, always listening.

Later today or maybe tomorrow, do exactly the same thing again and you could find you get some different variations or you might pick a different walk that feels most 'right'. If that happens then you can be sure that you are listening to *now* and not letting your head get in the way and tell you what it was or what it should be.

Still on walking, but you may not be able to do this straightaway… when you are out somewhere and your route takes you up a hill steep enough so that you find you're breathing a bit harder and maybe your legs feel a little strain… try changing *how* you are walking. There will be a best speed and a best style for *this* hill on *this* day feeling like you do at *this* moment. It might not be just slower - if we go too slowly we lose momentum and have to make more effort - and it may mean you have to notice at which point in your stride you need to 'push' and which point to relax, even momentarily, but you will know when you get it, because you'll feel you are in the rhythm (or the groove).

~~~

The two rhythms which are most vital to our existence are the beating of our heart and the passing of our breath. Physiologically we can manage, for a short while at least, without most other activities in our bodies, but not those. Most of the time we pay little attention to either, but if we do, it is our breathing that we mainly think about. That said, it comes into our mind most often when we are short of it rather than in terms of how it could help us. Long breaths, the standard instruction for someone in a crisis with anxiety, is about as far as we go. But in the context of our present quest our breathing means so much more.

So to start: without changing anything, for a couple of minutes, notice how you breath.

"In and out".

Ok, but *how*, in and out? Is your breathing smooth or do you find you randomly hold your breath? Are there pauses between the in-breaths and the out-breaths? Do your breaths seem short or long? Do you breath high or low, into your chest or into your diaphragm? Does your breathing feel steady or quite variable? Do you notice how much your breathing changes?

We can use breathing awareness as a tool. Later I will talk about breathing as a channel into meditation, but for the moment notice how you can use your breathing to reset that balance and help the Flow. From this point now, whenever you notice that your thoughts have strayed from what you were working with in your mind, or some discomfort has come on because of a situation you are in, or you're starting to give yourself a hard time for something you've done... turn your attention to your breathing, 'listen' to your breathing, 'follow your breathing'... and as you do that, take two *slightly* longer and *slightly* slower breaths, continuous breaths turning smoothly at the end of each... following the breath as if you were watching the air passing into your lungs and passing out again. As you come to the end of the second out-breath go back in your mind to where you left off, you will be able to start afresh. You may have to repeat the exercise, but the more you get used to doing it, the less disruption you will get and the less you will have to think about it as a routine. It will simply happen.

Shunryu Suzuki, a Zen master, likened our breathing, (in the way our out-breath follows our in-breath and our in-breath follows our out-breath), to a swinging door, the divider that doesn't really divide, between the inner world and the outer world - which are really one world, for the same air is everywhere for all of us, inside outside and around. The air we breathe knows no boundaries.

Our breathing has a rhythm, marked by the turning points of in and out. We can listen to our breathing and we can be aware of each turning point - a momentary stillness - as a meeting, an exchange.

......now the tune

In *Musicking* terms tune and rhythm can only exist together - they are mutually dependent... the rhythm has a beat and the tune has a rhythm. But 'tune' in Musicking has a pretty broad scope. We've already said that Musicking doesn't just include what we conventionally think of as 'musical', it also includes-*poetry and dancing and making faces, and swirling your*

*arms about and standing on one leg, and waving wistfully as
your friend's train pulls away* -and doubtless many I've
missed or which are still waiting to be discovered. All
of these expressions of feeling have a form and it's this
form we will call their tune. So, poetry has words and
rhyme (or non-rhyme), dancing has movement and
choreography, making faces has... well... melting
moods, swirling your arms has circles and a swing...
you see what I mean. And each have an underlying
rhythm.

Do you think you can get into this?

Here's how -

∼ take a large piece of plain paper and choose a pencil
 or a crayon or something that can draw

∼ play your favourite song or piece of music

∼ don't listen to the words or the tune specifically, but
 let your mind loose to drift with the music

∼ now take your pencil or crayon to the paper and
 'draw' your music in lines and swirls and dots and
 anything that comes

Try it a few times, use colours perhaps, and change the
music too.

What is this doing? It's helping you to make a direct
connection between what you are receiving (the music
playing) and what you are experiencing - the music
represented through and by and within you.

We can link our breathing into this as well.

Take the picture representation that appealed to you
the most, prop it up in front of you and look at it
intently, in a sense, 'watch' it. Be aware of your
breathing in the background, keeping it as smooth and
steady as possible and sense its gentle rhythm. After a
few moments start to play the music in your head as

you follow it on your drawing. Let your breathing loose to respond empathically to the music… it might seem to swell up as the sound builds, be steady and firm alongside a purposeful beat, almost quiver in a soft and thoughtful passage. Our breathing can resonate the music like this unnoticed anyway, and as we become aware of this what we discover is ourselves, because we are the link between what we receive and what we express.

There is no need to stop with one exercise or one tune, because perhaps this could tempt you to broaden your repertoire, try different songs, different styles. Then, when you really want to push the boat out, pick classical if your usual taste is pop, or pop if your usual taste is jazz, or rap if your usual taste is classical… or any switch you can think of, because this is not about becoming a devotee of different music, it is about feeling and expressing yourself with all parts of your being in the immediacy of what is happening right now. And if it ends up being the way you do a meditation, that's just fine too!

……now join in

True, you've been joining in already - I hope!. You've let in what has come into your orbit - yes, it was music, but it could have been a picture, or a view, or a meal, or a joke at the bar - and you've connected with your feelings and emotions in a way which has meant you could reveal them to yourself (and probably reveal them to anyone around)… but Flow means that you would also put something into the mix yourself. No, it's not scary, we do it all the time, but the difference now is that what comes will be from the most 'up to date' part of you, from the feelings which have just arisen (maybe are still arising) out of what you've just- *heard, seen, tasted, smelt, touched* -and which you've learnt to be able to express. If you've done the exercises as described, with no *thinking-about-what-you-were-supposed-to-be-doing* or *thinking-about-whether-you-were-doing-it right* getting in between the music and your artwork and your breathing, then at these instants, now, whatever comes from you will be as REAL as it gets... so long as you don't let thinking get in the way.

> *Department meeting. She dreaded them. So repetitive, all of them taking their usual positions, all of them bringing in their usual gripes, pushing their usual agendas and they'd all go away again and simply carry on. Because nobody listened. But what was the point of listening because you'd heard it all before? Perhaps this morning She should say something different just for the sake of it. Just to see if anything could change. But it wouldn't work. No, just sit quiet and try not to be noticed.*

What did *you* do?

Did you hum your tune? Did you wave your arms? Did you tap the table to the beat of your heart? Did your eyes dance?

Did *you* keep it Flowing?

SOLO 2

and the harmony

·

Harmony, musical or not, is about relationship. Generally we just know when life feels right, whether that's because things have just resolved themselves into the most desired outcome, or whether there's a feeling that events are moving in the right direction and it's only a matter of time before everything falls into place. We can get this sense with music and we can get it with romance and friendship and work and fitness, there's that feeling of a comfortable passage and that release from letting things simply work at their own pace.

We are in the flow.

Of course there is never certainty - the music suddenly stops or ends on a discord, the friendship becomes distant, work is a struggle, we are interrupted by illness or injury - but while they last there is a quality and a feeling about those periods of harmonious progression which is quite distinct. And if we looked inwards, we would notice that we have a different sense of the person we are too. This person is relaxed, is kindly, and smiles at the world around because for them the world around is basically ok - their default mode is to accept, and allow, and to let this world be as it is.

But when it is not like this, a whole different set of mechanisms operates. In place of 'letting' comes 'telling'; in place of allowing comes suspicion; in place of accepting as the default, comes reluctance, we attach conditions to our cooperation, demands perhaps. Most of us would squirm if someone suggested we were 'controlling' (and it's an extreme word) - our reflex response "that's not me" - but sure enough our feeling of ease has given way to a wariness and fault-finding which colours our meetings and our interaction with others.

We can get a feel for the difference with a short visualisation...

> Imagine for a moment that you are the first and only human being on the planet, at least that is how it seems. In your primeval bewilderment, it is almost as if you don't exist, because you don't exist as 'something'... there is no category of thing you can see that you can put yourself into... you look down at the ground - rocks and stones - but you're not one of those because they are inert... you look around at the trees - they're not inert, they sway in the wind, but they are fixed in one place, so you can't be one of them... look carefully among the trees and you catch sight of the gleaming eyes of wild creatures, they are not fixed, anything but, yet you're not one of them either because you walk upright on two limbs...

What are you feeling right now, as your primeval self?

> Suddenly you notice, coming down the hillside on the other side of the stream something standing upright, waving two arms like your's, its head looking out not down on the ground... more and more similarities... smooth appearance with hair just in places... and now it dawns on you... "That's it! I'm one of them"...

What are you feeling right now as your primeval self?

> The 'one of you' is coming closer now, only the stream between you... it's waving its arms around very vehemently... you can hear the noise it's making... now you see it's bigger than you and it looks quite strong... and now it's seen you...

What are you feel now as your primeval self?

So what was happening there?

If you followed the visualisation 'in role' I imagine you felt relief and a lift in your spirits when you saw the 'one of you' in the distance - something making sense, having a place now - immediately you are welcoming (even though you knew very little about it), your underlying assumption that it was ok.

But this changed as it got closer and you noticed more about it. You could feel anxiety growing - now it started to be not so much 'one of you' as a thing a bit like you but different from you. The change, though, was not in the other creature, the change was in you, not because it was closer and you could see it better (though that was true), but because, as your euphoria dissipated, the creature slowly slipped from being the completely ok other 'one of you' into being a thing, an 'it' that you could not be sure about.

So you think the whole visualisation and role-play was a bit far-fetched. Perhaps, but it touches on one of the most fundamental philosophical questions humankind has ever sought to resolve - what do we mean when we say 'I'? Or, as we could ask it, "Which 'I' am I right now?"

There are only two possibilities and they were both in your role play. One I is the I who accepts the other as ok (yes, without knowing all the facts, so has to trust) and will take another alongside; and the other I is the I who stands off, observes, formulates and defines their idea of what or who the other is, waits to see perhaps, but in the meantime keeps its distance.

Martin Buber was a philosopher who gave these two versions of 'I' names, he called them 'I-Thou' (the first one, the accepting one) and 'I-It' (the defining one). He wrote in German and 'Thou' was the closest way that the idea of 'you' as an individual acting and being alongside me, could be translated into English without the confusion of whether the 'you' was singular or plural, subject or object.

You could be excused for wondering if this is not a distinction without a difference and so cannot really have more than semantic significance. But it lies at the heart of our attitudes to each other, and anything that does that, affects all our relationships. That's important because it is relationships that are what we human beings are about, for few of us live alone on an island and even those that do are unlikely to be completely self-sufficient. Even so, perhaps it seems that specifically the 'I' bit cannot really make that much difference.

But let me play you another scene:

You are walking down the street and as you come round a corner you see three people coming towards you (there are actually four, but you don't notice the fourth till later), they are younger than you, two men and a woman, talking and laughing, loud, dressed black, "no doubt with piercings" you think, quite dishevelled, flamboyant body language, taking up a lot of space (physically and metaphorically). The walkway should be wide enough to allow you to pass, but you are feeling some discomfort - are they going to confront you, not let you through - which way to go round, squashed up against the wall, or step into the road? You step into the road, a long way into the road, round a parked car in fact. On the pavement again you glance back to check they haven't stopped... that's when you notice the little boy - 5 maybe 6 at the most - pulling excitedly at his Dad's sleeve and pointing, and his Dad bending down and lifting him onto his shoulders so that he can see the football game in the park.[1]

How little information we take in before we make our judgement and cast the other as, well, 'them'! How tiny the fragment of the picture we need in order to fill in the rest with our stereotypes and assumptions!

Which I?

The 'I' we are using when we do that sort of thing, said Buber, is I-It. (Or I-Them) And this is the 'I' we are being whenever we start even describing in our mind what (or even who, sometimes) the other person is. And

---

[1] The inspiration for this cameo came from a poem by the American poet CK Williams called "Instinct", which can be found in his *New and Selected Poems*.

it matters because we change what we do and how we react according to what this 'I' has seen... or thinks it has seen. Remember, you went into the road, probably with a worried, if not slightly disapproving look, on your face, when you could have smiled at the little boy (if you had just noticed him) and exchanged a knowing glance with his father. That 'I' would have made a connection, but the other one put up a barrier.

Of course we do modify our ideas about people as we get to know them, but we're always playing catch-up, not just because we tend to hang on to our first impressions until we are really sure, just in case, but also because, by the time we do finally change our mind the other has had another, hour, day, week, month, year even, of their life go past with whatever changes that has brought. So, not only do we never get to *seeing* the person as they really are, we are never *interacting* with the person as they really are: we never know them 'right now' (those mindfulness words again).

Is there another option? 'I-Thou' said Buber. But that is a lot more difficult.

Here are the conditions we have to satisfy to be able to claim that "The I that I am using is an I-Thou":

- ∼ I am completely open to the other person being *all* of the person they are
- ∼ I am seeing and listening to them without letting any assumptions get in the way
- ∼ I know that they are human and have vulnerabilities (and in that I am just like them)
- ∼ They are OK

It's a big ask.

This list, encapsulating I-Thou, is the most resonant single theme making up our Flow, for it both works outwards in our relating to others and inwards in our understanding of ourselves. Yes, our 'I' can be I-Thou in the way we look at ourselves too.

It is not possible to feel I-Thou in all our relating all of the time - it would slow down many work and everyday situations, for a start - but to be there in most of our social and family interactions would make a very big difference for any of us. And even to have the wisdom of I-Thou available, so that we could consciously move there when it felt something else was needed, would smooth many rough passages. Most arguments are marked by the labelling of the other side as 'them' and then neither side hears the other. We may hear the words (perhaps) but the feelings - the fears, frustrations, frailties lying beneath - those we cannot hear and will go unheeded.

The first task of any mediator, couples counsellor or negotiator is to listen and so move each party themselves towards listening to each other, for it is the listening - genuine listening that first requires openness - which will have ceased long before.

So it is for us with ourselves. Depression follows lowered self-esteem, itself the product of self-indoctrination as "a failure" or useless or weak, verdicts which slowly acquire a certainty through the closing off which filters out all contradictory messages and leaves us listening only to what confirms our self-denigrating assessment.

The ability to shift our 'I' to I-Thou, whether for ourselves or the world outside, to consciously apply this for much of our day and to keep it available for the rest, is what I meant earlier when I referred to 'Levelling'. It is to put ourselves on the same level as another person and it says that whatever might be our differences of opinion or philosophy or culture or ethnicity or sexuality or religion or age or gender... perhaps you can find a few more... there is this sense in which we are of equal worth.

But yet more than that... we do not even see a difference because our relating - not the words we have to use to function, but our real relating - is on a feeling and emotional level, it is the shared experience of being human and vulnerable. In any relating going on between two people, the experience of each is different, but for each there is a process of which and in which the other is co-creator, giving and receiving. There are different layers: one layer is the layer that would be visible to anyone else, namely, talking and body language; but another layer is the 'holding' of the other in their esteem, their mindfulness of them in fact, which might be felt as liking or love or prizing, but does not need a special warmth, and may be more like respect or approbation, and all of these are present and playing a part, the hidden strands of the process of engagement, the metaphysical aspect of the meeting.

The Flow, in the way we are using the term here, happens at this process level. The word 'process' connects us with the idea of flow because it's the same word as 'proceed'. Likewise we talk about living as being what we are experiencing, and this as the continual and continuous movement (or procession) of our feelings.

In contrast there is a sense in which our thinking is static (the very opposite of process) and instantaneous - not the act of thinking (which is simply articulation), but the thoughts our thinking lights on. These are fixed, and so the 'I' which expressed them can only be an I-It. I-It can never truly flow, because it defines and holds fixed, and any movements are disjointed shifts of perception.

If we asked our mind to tell our story, it would give us an account of events and our reactions to them, of our development and what had happened to us, and all of this would be expressed in the past tense. But if we asked our body to tell our story, it would tell us what is happening now and what it feels like being alive in this present. The 'here and now' of mindfulness.

If you want to help your shift towards I-Thou, spot how much time you spend talking in a past tense and then make yourself use the present tense: it won't work all the time, but when it does, if you listen closely inside, you will feel a change.

Our body cannot tell us where we've been, only where we are.

And so we return to mindfulness, this time as the experience of being in the Flow, with I-Thou symbolising a form of mind-body.

SOLO 3

now between us............

I n the same way as we default to the object way of looking at things because we are almost always in our I-It mode and lose sight of the possibility that our experience of living could be very different if our default was the I-Thou mode, so we also take for granted that speaking is the necessary channel for human communication. And perhaps it seems that talking is 'born into' being human in a different (more fundamental?) way than being musical. After all, aren't there many more people who would say of themselves that they are not musical than are unable to speak?

But we cannot say with certainty whether language or music came first. The first musicking may have been a mother of an early *homo* species cooing to her newborn infant. Certainly the first sounds our ancestors produced (a long way short of language) will have had the immediacy of mindfulness: they will have been prompted most likely by pleasure or danger. It is also possible that the *neanderthal* species, which coexisted with successive lines of the *homo* species (the last of which was our own *homo sapiens*) and finally became extinct about 30,000 years ago, were more 'musical' for their last 100,000 years than *homo sapiens* alongside. It could be that the neanderthals' less community-based social structure meant less sophisticated demands for language development and more space for the development of what we might more readily call musical expression. There are indications that the *neanderthals* may have been 'musical' earlier than *homo sapiens*, and even of their perfect pitch.[2] If these social differences imply that music is rooted in the individual's need to express themselves for themselves, and language in their need to express themselves for others, then it validates our project here to incorporate musicking and mindfulness into the concept of a Flow of being.

All in the Breath

Binding music and language into our musicking mindfulness is our breath.

The earliest known musical instrument (generally agreed) is a bone flute about 30,000 years old... and it was the flute in its many forms which has offered humankind the easiest route to melody.

Breath is needed both to play a flute and to speak, but the significance goes further.

The earliest depiction of language was pictograms, or stylised pictures. When they were 'read' each formed a

---

2 Much of the preceding follows Steven Mithen in "Singing Neanderthals" (see bibliography).

complete word, a one-to-one correspondence between the sound and what is depicted. Pictograms gave way to ideograms, which conveyed qualities rather than physical resemblance, but still related on a one-to-one object rather than a sound basis. When written communication moved in the direction of individual letters with the early semitic forms of inscription around 1000BC, it retained a similar object orientation through the development of letter systems composed entirely of consonants, that is, the verbal mechanism of *stopping* breath, and had no symbols for the *attributes* of the breath.

Now, in an age when what was written down was most often read out loud, likely in a group where some others couldn't read, but also for individual reading, what the symbols represented being only partly defined it was for the reader-speaker to interpret what was written and convey it through the addition of breath sounds which carried his own particular definition.

In a sense the breath was the final carrier of meaning.

Over time dots came to be added to represent breath movement (ancient Hebrew and Arabic), but even so the original writer's full meaning was only transposed into readable form with the coming of letters to represent individual and *differentiated* breath tones… and so vowels were born!

Breathing, the original creator of melody in music. Breathing, the ultimate creator of meaning in language.

We are stumbling into the enigma that is our breath.

Stop for a moment and try to get your head round what we call BREATH. We loosely think of it as 'air'. But air is not breath until we breathe it. We cannot keep it, we can only hold onto it for a very limited time, then we have to give it back, slightly changed, and trust that something outside us will reset the changes we have made and maintain it in a form that will sustain our life.

It is what we need at the very beginning of our life and what we relinquish only at the very end. It is the fundamental process… proceeding… of our existence and it allows us to create beauty in melody and beauty in poetry.

The thirteenth century Sufi poet Jalal ad-Din Muhammad Rumi wrote a poem "Only Breath"[3]:

> *Not Christian nor Jew nor Muslim,*
> *(sunni or shia)*
> *Not Hindu,*
> *Not Buddhist, not sufi, not zen,*
>
> *Not any religion or cultural system.*
>
> *I am not from the East*
> *or the West, not out of the ocean or up*
> *from the ground, not natural or ethereal,*
> *composed of no elements at all.*
>
> *I do not exist,*
> *am not an entity in this world or the next,*
> *did not descend from Adam and Eve,*
> *not part of any origin story.*
>
> *My place is placeless, a trace of the traceless.*
> *Neither body nor soul.*
>
> *I belong to the beloved.*
>
> *I have seen the two worlds as one*
> *and that one I call to and know,*
>
> *first, last, outer, inner,*
>
> *only that*
> *breath-breathing human,*
> *being.*

---

[3] This version is based on a translation by Coleman Barks, which in turn is an adaptation of the original Farsi text to enable a Western reader to associate more easily with its meaning.

With our breath we create the Flow through our musicking and through our Dialoguing.

The Nature of Dialogue

The word itself, dialogue, designates two - two people, two sides, two-way, two voices, two parts. So why do we so often approach it as if there's only one, which naturally is usually me?

Compare these three versions of 'dialogue' on the same topic:

P(eter):   I have never believed that the Press should just be able to print what they wanted, regardless of whether it affronts public decency or security or privacy, or is even true sometimes. Fake news! And as for all this tapping into people's telephones and emails and the like. It's always justified in the name of getting at the truth and not letting officialdom get away with anything. They're so full of themselves as well - "public interest", that's the usual one, but who decides what the public interest is? They do, of course.

~~~

P(eter):   The Press really get to me sometimes. I don't know what you think, but they're always taking the moral high-ground and claiming public interest if they just want to print something that will sell a few copies because it's a scandal or a bit salacious or catches someone out. It doesn't seem to matter whether something is sensitive or who's going to get hurt - just do it if it sells copies.

P(aul): It seems sometimes like we want to shoot ourselves in the foot, but perhaps as a general principle things being out in the open is right regardless?

P(eter): You mean the truth just because it's the truth? And what about national interest and protecting the public, giving away secrets. No, that's being blind to consequences. They just fuel issues by giving a platform for anybody with a grudge and the way it comes over, it sounds as if the whole world's on the same side.

P(aul): I suppose it might help public sentiment when there's a way for people to feel they have been able to air their grievances.

P(eter): And that's the trouble - it's just an invitation to complain and there's no one moderating things... the journalists want a scoop, the editors want to sell papers, the owners want prestige, the Press Council, well, we don't hear much from them do we?

~~~

P(eter): The Press have always worried me in the way they seem to think they can print everything. Of course I know we have this cherished belief in the freedom of the Press in a democratic society, but sometimes it seems to go too far. Like when they hack into the private emails or phone of a government minister, for instance.

P(aul): But there must have been instances of things being revealed which needed to be revealed. Things like expense accounts.

P(eter): OK, there are things like that. But when they pry into people's private lives and sometimes false accusations are made. People get hurt. And public security can be put at risk.

P(aul): If only we could have some kind of completely independent vetting body that we would all agree to trust.

P(eter): The 'freedom of the press' just seems to put people at risk. It goes with 'democratic society', but in a democratic society people don't all agree.

P(aul): So perhaps it comes down to - what is the best we can do?

These examples illustrate three types of 'dialogue' which we could call -

> dialogue which in fact is monologue
>
> dialogue which is pretending
>
> dialogue which is genuine

The first two we are all guilty of more often than we probably would care to admit. The third is a form of dialogue which would certainly win us more friends, even if it does not necessarily influence people.

The first of the examples barely tries to pretend it is dialogue, because it is clearly simply a set of rigid opinions being delivered to a stooge who is not going to be given the opportunity to reply.

The second gets closer to dialogue because Peter lets Paul in by giving him enough of a gap to put a word in, but then immediately quashes his offerings by re-asserting his own view without acknowledgement of any other possibility, and then even goes further.

The third is genuine dialogue, which allows relating to happen because Peter not only gives spaces for Paul, but actually listens and acknowledges his points and even shows some flexibility in his own position.

If we were Paul, it is pretty certain we would prefer the third experience. We would feel listened to and included, and we would also listen in our turn. More important, we would feel better about ourselves *and* about Peter, and this regardless of our respective views. Peter's approach this time has dramatically increased the possibility of consensus.

So we must conclude that relationship has more mileage than intransigent opinion.

In our interchanges with others, there are two sorts of responses which indicate that our 'I' is I-It, namely, criticising and telling. They sound a bit similar, and they both contain the subtext "this is how it is" or even "I know and I am right", but the first is likely to be felt as a put-down and the second as a challenge. Both, though, put any hope of a relationship firmly on hold until the mood music changes, for each anchor their respective sides in an I-It. And that is crucial and counter-productive - because relationship has more mileage than intransigent opinion.

The characteristics of the third example approach the nature of the I-Thou -

- each has an openness to the other in what they are engaged in at that moment
- each is listening and receiving the other's views and working with them
- in doing this there is an unspoken acknowledgement that the other's process is important

If you are minded to, you could role-play each of the three examples in your head as each player in turn (yes, Paul is in the first one too - he is being told and not given a chance to speak). At the end of each run-through pause and ask yourself, as the character you are playing, what feelings you are left with and what those feelings might prompt you to say or do next.

Meeting

At the point of greeting, or of opening a conversation, or the point where one person might give way to the other, there is a meeting.

What will you make of the meeting?

What will you make of your very next meeting when you put this book down?

What would it take to have no expectations and no preconceptions (about yourself as well, of course, not just the other person)? That would be the mindfulness way. It would also be the way of Flow - nothing in play except what is contained in this present.

Many things could happen, but let's presume a simple greeting, you first, open, free from distractions and intrusions, the other not so much - offhand, distracted or distressed, you can't be sure. How to respond? It could be "See if I care", or it could be "Something up?". The first draws a boundary line - Keep Out! - the second stays in the meeting, with hope.

Meeting implies a line between, perhaps not as tangible as a boundary, but the place where something changes, where one thing ends and another begins, and also where connection transcends enclosure, and nonchalance transforms into interest. Physically it's easy, one thing ending, another beginning. I can reach out and touch another person and I know that I am touching a person who is not me. Metaphysically it is more complicated and Dialoguing is an aspect of the metaphysical (even though it is attached to the physical). Contained within our speaking exchanges are:

> our mood
>
> our experience of the surroundings
>
> our agenda
>
> our experience of the other
>
> our conventions with the other

These are the intangibles, some of them immediate, some of them less so, some more vividly in our awareness than others. They can be present as what they are and we may still be mindful - in fact, to consciously alter any would make our exchange less genuine... and genuineness is also an aspect of mindfulness. But just to be conscious that they also affect the nature of the Flow, will be beneficial.

The Three Scenes for Dialoguing
... with ourselves... with others... with nature

Our dialoguing with ourselves is in meditation, but dialoguing through meditation largely loses its link with dialogue in a spoken way.

Our meditation begins with mindful attention to our breathing... flowing without pausing, at first lengthened then gradually brought to an even normal rate like descending the gentle slope of a hillside and coming into a clear space, where we are able to simply be, where nothing needs to be defined and where nothing needs to happen, not even waiting, because waiting anticipates time which is to come, and in the simple being there is neither coming nor going.

Our exchange is with ourselves, our minds empty of intention so that our butterfly thoughts can float silently around and away, leaving the silence becoming stillness. The paradox of stillness and flow. For there is always flow within us and around us. My senses bring me something from the world around and even if that thing is 'inanimate', within me somewhere I respond... a closed door - and I feel secure or I feel shut out or I feel curious or I feel apprehensive... an open door - and I feel anxious or I feel hopeful or I feel chilly... always within me I make a response.

Now our breathing holds the clear space, with our body and our mind as one, the pulsing of our heart and the rhythm of breathing, connecting us to the world and being in the world. What comes into the stillness now, we acknowledge as the Flow, which we can feel as part of who we are, carrying and being carried, inner and outer, as the door gently swings.

We can be the I of our whole being and we can be the I who knows our being, observer and observed as one, but held in relation. We can be speaker and listener, seer and seen, the divinity of the purest I-Thou - together we are the actor of our being.

We can come to the others with whom we share our world and let them be the part that we are not, joint players of the scene, different in their many ways but sharing in this being, Thou to our I. With I-Thou we make a commitment - to be separate (for if we were not separate there could not be relation) and hold precious our common humanity. The Flow is the continuing process of reciprocation between us, which produces a stream of learning and offering and trusting and risking, as its melody sings through the hoping and the striving, the helping and the supporting.

~~~

There is another scene for I-Thou.

Our species has a home which we must share. We may try to burst the bounds of earth and we may be able to look down on ourselves from outside our planet-home, but in the end this earth is where we must stay, homebound. It is our destiny to be *part* of a larger body for we are simply one of almost 9 million species on earth of which around 1.2 million are animals, but we are neither the most numerous (ants), nor the oldest extant (horseshoe crab), nor the largest (bowhead whales)... the list of our non-supremacy goes on. So perhaps it would make more sense to see ourselves as a cog in the machine rather than the motor itself, or, more aptly, a cell in our planet's body not the life-giving force... not vital, like the air which everything living breathes in some way... not even any kind of super-intelligence which can 'manage' the planet, because in the end our intelligence with all its contrivances cannot manage Nature, which assimilates everything.

We cannot look on our human intelligence as 'outside the box', as if our ingenuity will always be able to find ways to push beyond the planet's cordon. So better, surely, to follow the path of dialogue in this too.

We would not be able to view the planet simply as a resource if our 'I' was genuinely I-Thou.

One late summer afternoon I was coming down from the forest ridge on my way back home at the end of a familiar walk, the rough track running between scrubland on one side and the occasional meadow of coarse grass on the other. The sheep were higher up in the mountains at that season and there was a blanket of emptiness all around. I was walking looking ahead, because for me there is always a romantic allure about paths which disappear into the distance, when I heard a swishing a little way away in the meadow. The sound wasn't any kind of intrusion, it was more like a new theme which emerges from nowhere as the orchestra subsides to a pianissimo. A young stag was galloping away down towards the stream; he crossed the stream, and I was hoping he would stop just on the other side so that we could share a moment simply being in each other's gaze. He didn't, he went into the thickets and trees which lined the water's edge a little further along and I lost sight of him. There he stopped and must have turned towards me, and he barked. I stood stock still, hoping he would show himself, and a little miffed because I was playing my part (I thought) by simply waiting... but he was angry! Now, young stags have loud barks and tend to let rip, let up, let rip, let up and soon enough move off. But this one was truly angry. His barking was continuous, becoming more of a roar. I stood my ground motionless for over five minutes, but I could not will him to be peaceful. Finally I resumed my walking, slowly, and he was very quickly silent. Then after a few seconds a loud grunt. Thank you? No, probably not. But a dialogue of sorts and each changed the other's flow - he, my mood, for I was pensive all that evening; I, his peaceful grazing, perhaps he lay down somewhere different to sleep.

With Nature there can be no dialogue. Nature (capital 'N') is simply the mechanism by which a limited and fixed resource (the planet) adjusts to imbalances introduced by external forces (asteroids occasionally) or internal components (humans frequently) in order to preserve its mass. But nature (small 'n') as we normally conceive it, is the amalgam of all the 'components' (including us) which are available for adjustment within that mechanism and interact to maintain an equilibrium. Neat and circular. But humankind has broken out of the circle. Unique species with consciousness (or at least, uniquely-nuanced consciousness), it can see beyond its present, make comparisons and define objectives. Believing itself supreme, it was of course not possible for it to enter into genuine dialogue but, taking its stance as I-It, has seen the planet in all its facets as its domain.

From I-It, mindfulness is impossible. Flow stops. Sensibility, consideration and respect come only with glimpses (at least) from I-Thou. And genuine dialogue, which has its own vindication in relation, has to start from there.

Was there relation between me and the angry stag? Of a kind, I think. Certainly there was consideration - for my part, I kept contact but gave way... for his, well, he didn't charge at me! - we each had respect for the other's space.

This solo ends here with an interrupted cadence... so far we haven't found a way to maintain the dialogue with the natural world and stay in contact... with my stag I probably never could... with the planet...

solo 3

SOLO 4

the drummer wants a turn

Iｆ you are reading this inside and if the weather is not too inclement, take yourself outside for a few minutes. Mostly when we find ourselves in the outdoors, we are either on our way somewhere or we are engaged in some outdoor activity - either way we are bound up in what we are doing. Usually that means we don't *see* anything other than what is requiring our attention and we don't *hear* anything at all!... unless we're making a noise ourselves. But we rarely get an impression of the sound of 'outsideness' because we seal ourselves off from everything which is not part of our immediate occupation. It happens automatically, that despite our incredibly extensive mental capabilities, we don't - we can almost say 'can't' - multi-task. Driving could be an exception - usually we can safely carry on driving while we are talking, so long as we keep our eyes on the road and don't look at the person we are talking to. We can also walk around holding a book and reading, so long as the cat doesn't get under our feet. But in these examples the repetitive part of our activity is being informed by a different part of our memory (the part which holds where it has literally just been.)

So today, right now, I would like you to go outside and just listen. Not scanning around for something to listen to. Just listen. And keep listening. Because it will take a few moments for your brain to re-tune to *not* trying to find something to attend to. Our minds are usually in a default state of looking and delving and that acts like a screen between us and the real world. So as you simply keep listening you are starting to part that screen... without any impulse to spy something on the other side, just to be on the other side. Anything you make out (hear) when you are there you can notice, but that's all... just notice.

When it feels like you have passed through the screen, and this may seem as if you are standing in a different space, then close your eyes. Be patient and let a 'scene' grow around you which in its ethereal intensity will be quite unlike anything else you know.

It can be a meditation.

If you find that a particular sound is drowning out the rest, you could think of it as pulling in your mind, inveigling it into giving it one hundred per cent attention, and your mind has succumbed and been hooked in by the din. If this happens simply unleash your mind from its captor and bring it back to where you need it to be, inside your body. Now the sound will be no more than *a part* of the scene.

To be able to hear without needing to 'listen to' is part of how we sometimes come to musicking. (Non-musicians can actually have an advantage here, because for many musicians it is difficult to simply hear music without attending to it in a technical kind of way.) With musicking, though, we don't need to *listen to* the music, mostly we can let it be like another person who is simply with us.

This notion of the music being like another person and that we can have a 'dialogue' with it when we are not ourselves playing might at first seem strange and so as an introduction I offer you this short meditation (5 minutes) which you can access on YouTube. There is a narration with a visual and, intermittently, there is flute music. The link is:

https://youtu.be/zz2jDJOkH_s

 I suggest you run it twice, both times treating it as a short meditation, the first time watching the screen, the second time with your eyes closed. Give yourself about 5 minutes each time after the narration (the screen will stay blank for this) simply remaining as you are. Then spend a couple of minutes bringing into conscious awareness the feelings that are with you from each run. (You might also jot these down.) Try it now.

The meditation offered you images, ideas, inspiration perhaps, and the thread of the melody. The *process* of linking all these, though, was within you. Even so, perhaps you thought that your part was just reactive, not really anything that felt like a dialogue. Hold that for now. Shortly I will suggest a way to extend your experience of this sort of meditation, but first we need to make a detour into process.

We use concept words to describe the sources of our big emotional states and for convenience we objectify them as if they were 'things' in their own right. So we have words like BEAUTY and FAITH and FREEDOM and MORALITY (there are many others), which evoke an emotional response. It can feel as if we could give them concrete definitions as 'things' so that our relationship with them can be explained, maybe even pre-ordained. In reality, though, for each one of us there is little that can be pre-ordained about such concepts, and across the plethora of human societies and cultures, nothing that can be said to be absolute.

We'll look at one of them. The most apposite to consider for our project here is BEAUTY. We talk of 'beauty' as if it were a 'thing' in its own right, and might go on to say that beauty resides in such and such a mountain view, or in a sunrise in the Sahara, or this or another cathedral, or the Taj Mahal... make up your own list. In reality, though, BEAUTY is a process. When we perceive something as beautiful it is anchored in our present experience. It is the object of our attention and it is specific to the moment in which we have the experience as the me which we are bringing into that moment. If we go back to a view or watch another sunrise or re-visit a place which inspired us, the light will have changed, and almost certainly some other aspect of the setting as well, and we will also have changed. We might still see it as beautiful, but our experience will be different If we look again at a painting our eye will be taken another way or our angle different and another detail stand out. Equally as ourselves, we come as a new person, an hour a day a year older, with an altered amalgam of experience and an altered perception. My perception of this or that as beautiful, therefore, is part of my process in the very present, a trace of my proceeding in the here and now, which cannot be separated from the human person that

I am and that I brought to that point. And it also alters in some way the me who moves on from there.

Beauty is a process not a thing.

In this way we are the orchestrator of our own symphony.

So go back and stand out in the open and be immersed.

The instruments, the notes, the range of sounds, of soft and loud, of fast and slow, are available, and we can select, arrange, transpose… compose.

Or, we can walk out onto the concert platform of living sounds, letting each be ok there because they *are* there, and allowing the symphony to compose itself, with harmonies dissonant and melodious and voices demure and strident and rhythms subtle and insistent… and somewhere a drummer keeping the beat.

Let me offer you another way to dialogue in another musicking meditation. You will hear my narration again and the flute, but this time no changing images, so you might close your eyes. It can be all sound… and silences. The silence is for you to fill, with actual sound if you wish, or in your head.

Back in the chapter 'Solo 1', you listened to your breathing as it responded to a favourite piece of music. This time, as you hear the flute come into the meditation, once again let loose your breathing to respond to the sound of the melody; listen for how it does this and let yourself go to the sound and be with it, now feeling it permeate deep into your body. The sense of this is something between awareness and symbiosis, the image maybe of early morning mist amongst the mountain trees before it's burnt off by the sun, the sensation a fuzzy tingling at the base of your spine. Soon the flute will stop and leave silence and you can respond with melody or harmony or the feeling of your spirit that simply comes... you may not make a sound, or perhaps you will - humming, tapping, singing, breath - or if you have a flute, whistle, recorder, drum by you - playing it, but not with any arranging in your head of what you are going to play, rather letting it speak as you. Now some more narration and then my flute will come back, but again it will leave a break for you to continue the dialogue. Finally I close with some more narration.

Here is the YouTube link:

https://youtu.be/zNaDkvGWuxA

In a similar way, perhaps you will be able to use musicking as a natural part of even a silent solo meditation. Whisperings arise in the clear space which we create with our breathing, whisperings which are not exactly thoughts, but more like glimpses, sounds half-caught, murmurs, flashes of memory... open yourself to these and let a feeling come up in response. The feeling might coalesce as a part of you, which you can allow to respond itself to what has arisen, so that what has arisen changes slightly and then the feeling may change slightly and now there is a dialogue emerging in the Flow.

This is the way shifts happen in meditation, and the way a path appears - through our openness to receive whatever comes simply because it comes.

Ibn al-Arabi (13th century Sufi philosopher and mystic) suggested that there are three kinds of knowledge - intellectual knowledge and information, which most of us use most of the time; the knowledge of (emotional) states, which leads us to self-awareness and a sense of

depth; and then there is the knowledge which those
find who reach that peace which is beyond the intellect
and the emotions.

MIXING IT

where's the tune ... keep it flowing

T he reason for putting so much emphasis on Flow is
that it is the very opposite of fixed, which is what we are
when we've given way to our fears and frailties and
when we believe that we lack the power to take hold of
our own life. In doing that, somewhere, we are holding
onto something which is not, or need not be, part of
our lives, not now. We are not being mindful, at least
not wholly mindful, because being wholly mindful
would be the first step in re-constructing that part of
our life which we had shackled with this stubbornness.

Flow is the opposite. Flow is movement. It also implies
direction. Those aspects of musicking we have looked
at - melody and dialogue - they both have direction.
Both feel as if they are 'going somewhere' and this
'going somewhere' must surely be an antidote for the
fixity which leads to distress.

This 'going somewhere' seems to be hard-wired into being human. Even though there may be times in our lives when we are conscious of 'being stuck', the very fact that we remark on being stuck, usually in quite a demoralised tone, indicates that our preferred experience is to be moving - going somewhere. I notice, as I am writing, that I am not wanting 'goal' or 'destination' to slip in, or anything less vague than 'somewhere'. That would be equivalent to sitting to do a meditation with an expectation that something *had* to happen.

But I do accept that 'going somewhere' does beg the question - where?

If that is a question you are asking, I instinctively want to reply "to the next going", because in reality there is nowhere to arrive, ever. Every step is a landing *and* a takeoff. And if we were able to scan ahead to find a destination we would be looking forever. Rilke, not always, I grant, the easiest of poets to understand, intimated this when he compared the animal's vision (the natural world) with the human, in his Eighth Elegy[4]:

> With all its eyes the natural world looks out
> into the Open...
> ...Free from death.
> We, only, can see death; the free animal
> has its decline in back of it, forever,
> and God in front, and when it moves, it moves
> already in eternity, like a fountain.

The paradox of our awareness of the certainty of our death, our ultimate arrival, is that we feel driven to set up for ourselves intermediate goals as if they could be certainties. But this 'going somewhere' has been with

4 Rainer Maria Rilke, from the Eighth Elegy, translated by Stephen Mitchell

us for as long as we can remember, so I want to offer
you a version of one of my themed meditations, to bring
you from as long ago as you can remember to this very
moment. Try it now.

Meditation : On Being Just Who I Am

We have lived these many years and we must
value all that they have brought.

We have trodden so many roads and still could
feel the buzz of starting here.

We have met so many others who have shaped
the one we are and all should have a place
because of who we are and because we must
respect the one we are, prizing our story for all its
many parts.

We cannot love others unless we love ourselves
and we cannot love ourselves unless we love this
person we are, here and now...

*Start with three long breaths and allow your out-breaths to
smoothe the tensions in your muscles so that you can feel your
whole body ease and relax...*

*Let your breathing subside into a gentle even rhythm as you
move into your clear space...*

*When you are at ease in your clear space, turn your attention
onto yourself, but don't look inward, rather see your whole
self, sitting as your are...*

*Allow a sense to develop of being both the observer and the
observed, seeing and being seen almost in the same instant...*

*Notice without judgment the different parts of you and how
they link to different aspects of your life, what is visible on
the outside and what only you know on the inside...*

*Treat everything that comes into your mind equally,
nothing is good and nothing is bad,
Here, now, everything is simply a part...*

*As you notice more and more parts of you, aspects of your
life, people you know past and present, each with a place in
your story, be aware of a sense of your parts as strands that
form together into a thread which winds through your life to
this moment now...*

*Let your sense of this thread of your life, you as the observer
and the observed, and where you are now, all merge to form
one image...*

*Listen for a feeling of ease within you, be patient and let it
come to you, dwell with it...*

*When you are ready, turn back to your breathing and
lengthen your breaths to bring yourself back into your room.*

~~~

You are the person standing at the end of your story so
far. You may be proud, you may be regretful. You may
be lively, you may be tired. You may be joyous, you may
be sad. You may be peaceful, you may be troubled.

But you are here, the only you.

Life is a succession of going somewheres and each one
leaves a trace, some leave more distinct marks, some
leave scars, but this person standing at the end of the
story is unique and has played their individual tune. If
you are someone who is more conscious of your past
than curious about your future, more readily aware of
the things that have gone wrong for you than hopeful
that things can go right, then ponder for a moment this
proposition - that in musicking the melody is always
unfinished.

Let's try and hear this.

Take any song or tune you like and play or sing or hum
or imagine the ending. Almost everyone will be able to
get a feel for a piece of music, any piece, coming to a

close. For musicians this is marked by a cadence and usually the most 'satisfying' cadence is the 'perfect cadence' with the dominant note or chord followed by the tonic. But whether you are a musician or not, when you play my next YouTube video, you will pick up what I mean by the feeling of a perfect cadence. It's a bit like a job well done, that satisfying and satisfied feeling. And if our lives were made up of a whole long series of perfect cadences it would certainly feel very rewarding and comforting. They aren't, of course, and so we get imperfect cadences and half cadences and interrupted cadences, but there's something about these other sorts of cadences - they all sound as if the music is going on from there.

Maybe there's a salutary lesson from all these different cadences...

the perfect cadence, the one which allows us to feel contented...

- if it's music it's the end, no need to go on, no more to say,
- if it's life, settle back, nothing more to do - but wouldn't that be a little bit boring?

the other cadences,

- in music in different ways they leave something unfinished as if there *is* more to hear,
- so in life, it's not the end, the beat hasn't stopped and the path leads on.

Play this YouTube video now and then we'll take this up again:

https://youtu.be/QyjasLVhCtk

Those non-perfect cadences all invite the flow to continue - you can hear how in different ways they are expectant of something coming. It can be like that in life too if we learn to sing our next note, continuing the Flow.

Can you bring to mind some time when life seemed to have gone wrong for you and you were left feeling stuck? Keep this in your mind and now also, as you think of that time, hear the tune, the one in the video, which doesn't really end but leaves you waiting.

Waiting is better than stuck, it's a comma not a full stop.

Now let the tune play on, in your head be the piper, make it up yourself, and feel the flow resume.

For this is what has happened, somehow, all those hundreds, thousands of times, to lead you to this point at the end of your story so far... the "thread which has wound through your life to this moment now" is the melody which has played in the background of your life, yes, with pauses, with interrupted cadences, with dissonances and shifts in key, sometimes fast sometimes slow, sometimes loud sometimes soft... but always there. The thread and the melody are the same.

The piper has kept on playing.

This is the contribution of *musicking* mindfulness, as the accompaniment to living, and, like every good accompanist, sensitive and responsive, interested and understanding, and always providing an opening.

~~~

Now play on...

There is another lesson that musicking teaches us, not in our face, we have to notice - that nothing is ever exactly the same the next time. If you play an

instrument you will recognise this straightaway, because
you will know there's always something different every
time, another mistake - oh no!-, or a slightly different
speed or a slowing down or speeding up, but also, if you
sing a song or hum a tune, you never quite repeat, not
exactly. Even listening to a recording another time…
are you in the same room, are you in the same mood?…
and if you dance or walk around, are these the same
shoes, are you on the same surface?

The Buddha said (but probably someone had noticed
before him): "Everything changes".

In "Pathways" I tell a story which has been around in
many different traditions for centuries. I will tell it here
too:

> There was once a king who was feeling very out
> of sorts, no, worse than that, more and more
> depressed in fact. He was often quite distressed.
> He ruled many lands and whilst he did not want
> his subjects' lives to be miserable - because he
> liked to have other rulers look on and be
> impressed by how he governed - nevertheless
> every last thing had to be carried out in the way
> that he decreed. Mostly things went well enough
> because his subjects were fairly settled - it was
> only occasionally that some revolutionary came to
> the fore and there started to be murmurings
> among the populace and then of course he had to
> deal with that, usually by 'disappearing' the
> troublesome person.
>
> Try as he might the king could not work out the
> source of his distress. He knew that he had
> everything set up perfectly. There was stability in
> the kingdom and if occasionally he had to make
> 'adjustments' in the interests of keeping everyone
> comfortable with their lives, well, that was just a
> minor inconvenience. So what was it he was
> feeling now? He wondered if it might be
> melancholy, though he couldn't see why, but he

was more and more prone to outbursts for no real reason at all.

In the end he called his wise men together and put the problem to them. He could not continue like this. It was necessary that he became happy again - for the good of his people, of course. He would give them a week to shut themselves off, to talk and to contemplate and to find a solution and bring it to him. And just in case they needed an incentive to come up with something effective, if they didn't come back to him with a solution in the time, then he would 'disappear' them.

The wise men were perplexed at the king's demand. They instinctively felt that with everything working so well in the kingdom the solution to the king's difficulties would not be found in changing anything that was around him, rather it would be within the king himself that any change would have to come about. But how to convey this to him… and be around long enough to see him get better? They worked hard, all night towards the end, and on the appointed day they presented themselves in the court. Nervously they offered him what they had prepared for him - an intricately carved ring. And their spokesman stepped forward to explain their gift to the king:

"Your majesty, it might seem like a very little thing to give to a king who feels such great distress, but this ring is a symbol of everything that life contains for each of us.

Firstly it is a circle, the perfect geometric shape, which shows us that everything is required for completeness and that no one part is more important than another.

Secondly we can look at the ring and see it as the form it is, a solid object; but we can also look at it and look through it and then it is like a moving window and what appears depends on how you are holding it.

And thirdly the ring has an inscription running around it, which has no ending."

At this the king looked at the ring and read the inscription and as he did so he began to feel his spirit slowly lifting.

It said: "THISTOOSHALLPASS"

Sometimes there is nothing we can do except wait, but we can wait with hope if we keep in our mind that everything passes. This is not the same as the ego does when it waits in expectation that something will appear "because something *should* appear". The waiting I mean here is waiting calmly, peacefully and openly. Openly - the opposite of the waiting with attitude we so often do... none of that impatience of waiting for a friend who is late, none of that exasperation because the queue is so long, none of that annoyance because the organiser should have introduced me first, none of that frustration because it was really my fault I was late... all of these and many more are 'waiting with attitude' and they all have one thing in common, namely, that we are closed off to everything else that's going on.

The waiting I am talking about is waiting mindfully... at this exact moment there is nothing else that I can do, but, *this too shall pass*. So long as I allow it to pass. Allow it to pass? Yes, because if I give way to impatience or exasperation or annoyance or frustration, I am fixing it as a thing, (I'm nowhere near I-Thou), and as a thing I've got it stuck... and I'll miss the change.

My examples may seem on the trivial side (but then most of the instances life gives us are trivial really), but the principal works for the big things as well.

Bring to mind the last time you suffered a loss, any kind of loss that really hurt, it could have been a death, or it might have been a relationship, or your job, or a pet, and recall the feelings that were around and most likely stayed around a while. You had to keep the wheels turning, but it might have felt as if you had hibernated, or the world had become like a black & white photograph, or nothing really registered and if it did it had no meaning anyway. You stopped noticing because nothing interested you, and you just existed.

And then one morning, much later, you were outside and you heard a bird singing and it almost startled you. You looked around and there were flowers. Little by little the world was breaking through again.

I don't know whether it could have happened sooner if you had known about the Flow or how you would use it now to sustain you. There is no miracle cure. But one morning you were open enough for the musicking, which is all around all the time, to be heard and felt.

And then that dark time, which might have come and seemed to last for ever, or maybe was what you knew as coming back and back again and again, when you feel hopeless and a failure because there is nothing you can make work, nothing you can get right, and everyone sees you as that pitiable figure. You feel useless and worthless and desperately unhappy. A very dark place where the world seems to close in on you like the sides of a deep pit. You have no belief in yourself and you 'know' that no-one else believes in you either or has any time for you.

In such a closed-off place you can only wait. But will you wait and be open? Will you wait simply hearing in your mind *this too shall pass...* and listening out?

Listening out, because somewhere the piper is still playing.

We will close this chapter with a themed meditation. This is a 'moving on' meditation. As before, the opening passage is to set the scene and then the narration of the sitting itself follows in italics.

Meditation : To Accept that Everything Changes

Change is constant, everywhere. There is no part of the universe which is not evolving. There is no living thing on our planet which is not developing and maturing.

We may sit and contemplate the mountain and feel grounded through its massive and seemingly unchanging presence, and yet what we see is relative to our timescale and lifespan.

We may look at ourselves and feel the comforting constancy of our sense of self, and yet our own body is composed of clusters of atoms in a frenetic dance of never-repeating relation.

We can never change that everything changes.

We can only engage with what is presented to us and awaits our response.

And we can choose.

What will *you* choose? For to choose being your only option, in making a choice you are creating *your* change, *your* path, each step along which is a process of evolving and a grain in the evolution of everything.

In choosing, you are creating your future. And you are touching the lives of others. For ever.

Sit quietly for a few moments, noticing the way your mind is bound by what you are doing...

Notice that even in noticing there can be a tenseness...

just BE here

Let your mind float away from the grip of this tension…

Like the early morning mist when it evaporates with the heat of the sun…

Under the open sky, the changing of things can be sensed…

The wind in the trees rustling the leaves and passing by…

Water in the stream cascading over its bed of stones and flowing on…

Clouds swirling through their gamut of shades and shapes, twisting, disappearing…

In your mind you can walk over an open field,

like the unfolding of your life as you pass along,

morsels of time approached seized relinquished,

a passage of living, meeting, adapting, renewing…

Play this picture in your mind, becoming used to the feeling of passing along…

New experiences always opening up…

The field a passage of living,

offering itself for your experience…

When you are ready, turn your attention to your breathing, which is always walking with you…

Feel it as your regular support, even and steady…

Little by little let your breaths be longer and firmer as you open yourself up to the room around.

mixing it

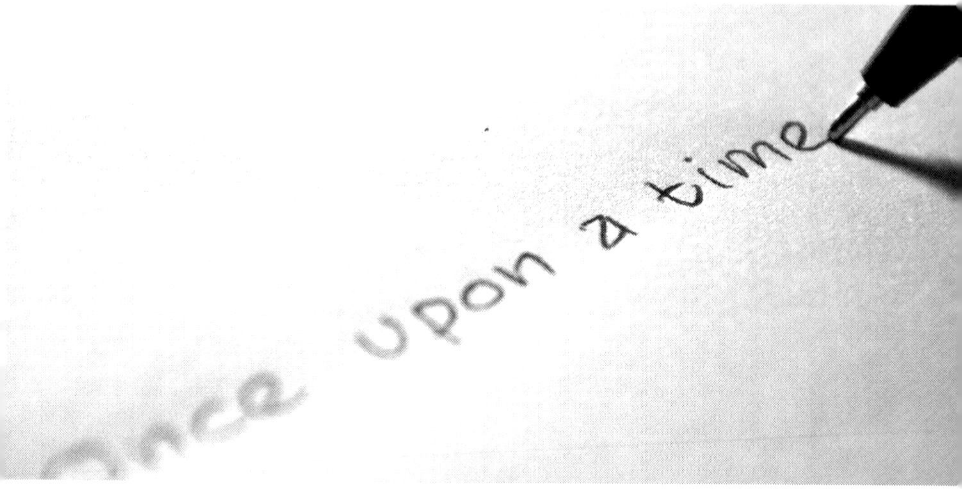
Once upon a time

CODA

the ending which doesn't need to

$\mathbf{I}$ t is usual, and therefore predictable, that 'teaching' books such as this conclude with exhortations to regular practice in order that the reader can ensure the maximum benefit from the time they have invested. I will offer some thoughts along these lines too, but what I have sought to provide in these few pages is not so much a life-enhancing bolt-on-extra (though perhaps you will feel enhancement) or life-changing ritual (though I hope you will feel a change), but a way to uncover what was there all the time, and in the process open yourself up to another dimension of living.

So, my thoughts on putting into practice first.

Really, I hope you already have. I have not set out to 'drill' you, but I do believe you will be motivated into the discovery of this special part of you, if you have paused and followed the exercises and experiments, as well as the meditations, as we have gone along. And I hope that you will have started to fit them into a framework - your own framework - that can become part of your life. And that is not just about exercises, of course, it is the way of thinking about this human living and feeling the Flow coursing through your life. As a shortcut to the practical parts and a summary of what you might have set up as bookmarks, the chapter following gives a recapitulation of the themes - not musically correct, of course, to put a recapitulation after the coda, but it felt like the way to respect the natural flow of this particular work.

It could be that you want to make a regular practice of mindful contemplation or meditation, with or without your own musicking input. The key to a regular practice of anything which you want to make part of your life is the first couple of weeks. I suggest you make a contract with yourself, such that, once you have 'signed off' on the deal, it is set for two weeks. This means that, not only will you not change it, but you will not even think about whether to keep to it or not, you will 'simply do it'. After the two weeks you can have a review and decide whether you feel benefit and wish to renew. (My hope would be that if it's going to work for you, by the end of the two weeks, you would feel there was something missing if you stopped.)

The key elements of the deal? Something like this:

- set a start time
- set a finish time
- set a place - comfortable, familiar, minimum distractions
- decide on your trappings - what you wear, what you sit on, anything you bring with you
- work out how you are going to start
- work out how you are going to finish

coda

There is no need to be too rigid, but you will benefit from being as consistent as possible during these first two weeks. Being rigid doesn't go with flow, but being consistent *does* help with developing routine. It will be a balance and, of course, it will be *your* balance.

In the end this is not about the practice of a routine or the adopting of a discipline, it is about the development of a way of being. It is not even about developing a replacement you, it is about uncovering what is already within you, and already functioning in some way, albeit stuttering and misfiring along the way. We could say that the circuits are all there, but the connections are only randomly being made.

You will have begun to see that the premise of musicking mindfulness as we have worked with it here is not that mindfulness is simply a state which we seek to achieve as an antidote to the busy-ness and pressures of living. Musicking mindfulness is a practice in which each of us is agent, contributing as much *into* the communal wellness pool as we might derive from it in being able to access for ourselves a condition of immediacy and connectedness.

If we think of an individual's mindful state as a thing, it is 'it', and therefore static, even if the awarenesses which it incorporates are not. This risks casting each one of us simply as receivers and that is not a natural condition in a species for which the primary mode of living is to relate and interact.

In the end (and despite this book's title) it is not enough to "just BE here", we also have to "simply DO it".

The Flow requires that we are constantly reciprocating, always in relation, forever meeting.

The three aspects of the Flow - Musicking, Dialoguing, Levelling - which we identified at the beginning, are all there as strands of our persona and manifest in different forms and with different strengths according to the individuals we each are. The strands exist together - they may seem like layers of liquids with different viscosities which mingle and coalesce but can always be distinguished, which has a spatial feel - they may seem like colours of different frequencies which, shining together, create a new light that still intimates its origins, more of a spiritual feel. How it is for each one of us is not pre-determined, so this is not about achieving a unique ideal state, but about finding an individual way.

Musicking has been the facilitator. It is everywhere but we need to recognise it. If we delve into ethnomusicology, we quickly find that we have to dramatically widen the scope of what we conventionally describe as 'music', and then we have to allow that seeing it simply as entertainment woefully understates the function of music around the world. It stands, though, as *a* universal communicator, if not *the* universal language, and so our usage here has been to borrow from this and see *musicking* as the interface between our inner and outer worlds, a passing through that gently swinging door.

Dialoguing can be the coding of that interface, the gritty basics that allow the interpersonal world to function, the workhorse of our relational existence.

Levelling defines how we start. It brings us to the meeting. It *is* the - Open Sesame! - for I-Thou reveals the world as it is, not how we think it is, and promotes the reciprocation and sharing which is the essence of being alive as a human.

coda

So that's it - just BE here - simply DO it
Whoever you are, wherever you go, I wish you well -
and listen out for the piper...

Recapitulation of Themes

Rhythm... solo 1

Start by just walking... across the room, down the garden

Now do it again and change the way you are walking... slower, faster, hip swing

And listen, that is, listen to how it is for your body

Now do it again, still listening, and change from one walking style to another... and start to feel the rhythm

Get used to tuning in to what it's like for your body when you are moving... walking uphill for instance, what speed and rhythm feels best inside?

Rhythm and Breathing... solo 1

Start by just noticing how you are breathing... short or long, fast or slow, steady or held up sometimes... and how and where do you sense your breathing?

Listen to your breathing to turn your attention away from irrelevant thoughts or to calm anxiety... simply turn your attention to your breathing, notice where your breath is going in your body, take two longer (down into your diaphragm) and slower breaths, then return to normal but steady breathing and go back to where you wanted to be in your mind without distractions.

Melody... solo 1

Listen to a song or some music that you like while sitting with a large piece of paper and a pencil, crayons, or felt tips... as the music plays start to draw on the paper, letting the shapes that come out have a feel of the music that is playing.

Melody and Breathing... solo 1

Sit with your drawing propped up in front of you and study it for a few moments allowing your breathing to steady and settle into its shapes... now start your music and continue to sit looking at your drawing and letting your breathing respond to the music, filling, growing, slowing, shortening... whatever comes.

Try all of these with different music... put on music and styles you would not normally listen to and explore them in a similar way.

Discovering 'I'... solo 2

Replay the scenario of being the only person on the planet and not knowing what you are... until a figure appears across the river and you notice your feelings as it gets closer, moving from elation to anxiety, from an impulse to join with it to keeping it at a distance.

Watch yourself watching others... at what point do you find you 'know' the sort of person they are, check yourself, go back, what might you not have seen, how much are you knowing and how much are you presuming?

Replay real interactions in your head but holding to your 'I' as I-Thou... notice any change in your feelings and how you feel about yourself, consider how it might have been different for the other person.

Dialogue and Meeting... solo 3

Replay your day and listen carefully to yourself in your exchanges with others... categorise your dialogue at significant moments into whether it has been:

> dialogue which is really monologue
> dialogue which is pretending
> dialogue which is genuine

Replay the Peter and Paul exchanges in your head, role-playing each of them in each of the examples.

Replay a conversation you have had with someone during the day; listen carefully to your part of the dialogue and notice how your words or phrases or tone of voice in various places have been affected by:

> your mood
> your experience of the surroundings
> your agenda
> your experience of the other person at that time
> your conventions with the other person

Consider the effect on the conversation and the other person if any of these had been different.

Process and Proceeding... solo 4

Go outside, close your eyes, and listen to the 'outsideness'... pass through the screen of looking and delving and experience the scene of sounds which forms, free from your intervention.

Use the video links to enhance your experiencing of the Flow.

just BE here

Bibliography

The following are some of the books and writers which have contributed to the thinking behind my approach here and have been alluded to in some way in the text, and which may be worthy of consideration for further reading.

Abrams, David: "The Spell of the Sensuous"

An anthropologist who turned to ecological philosophy and traced early development of language, and the relation and reciprocity between perception and terrain.

Buber, Martin: "I and Thou"

Hasidic Jew, philosopher, anthropologist, sociologist, Buber had an immense written output, amongst which "I and Thou" is the iconic philosophical work. All his works were written in German and many are fairly impenetrable. "I and Thou" is quite short and he suggested was written as an 'ecstatic utterance".

Cole, Simon: "Pathways: humanity's search for its soul"

'Lyrical philosophy' seeking to uncover the essence of being human. In the context of the present work, it is of relevance for an up to date rendering of the essentials of pt.1 of "I and Thou", as well as a chapter on the philosophy of Ubuntu, which has similarities to "I and Thou" from a very different culture.

Mithen, Steven: "The Singing Neanderthals"

An erudite examination of the early development of communication and the beginnings of language and music through the line of our distant ancestors.

Nettl Bruno: "The Study of Ethnomusicology"

A wide-ranging study of the geographic distribution of musical phenomena and the difficulties of intercultural comparison.

Oehrle, Elizabeth: "Creative Musicking - with African, Indian and Western musics"

Practical comparisons of musical conversing from different cultures and ethnicities.

Small, Christopher: "Musicking: the meanings of performing and listening"

A vivid and detailed look at the roles and experiences of the contributors to the musical exchange. Perhaps the first person since medieval English to put a 'k' on music for musicking.

Shunryu Suzuko: "Zen Mind, Beginner's Mind"

A wonderful example of how a Zen master talks and teaches. In the present work the source of the analogy of the swinging door.

The Author

Simon Cole has been a counsellor-therapist as well as meditation teacher for around 35 years across a wide range of medical and non-medical settings. He has also taught counsellor training programmes at all levels in an institutional context and in private practice.

He has worked in the UK, France and online with clients of many different nationalities and ethnicities from around the world.

Currently with his wife he runs a centre for residential retreats and therapy in south-west France.

email:	simon.cole.france@icloud.com
counselling and retreats:	www.life-counselling.co.uk
books:	www.stillnessinmind.com

For your creative flow...

For your creative flow...

For your creative flow...

For your creative flow...

For your creative flow...

For your creative flow...

For your creative flow...

For your creative flow...

For your creative flow...

Printed in Poland
by Amazon Fulfillment
Poland Sp. z o.o., Wrocław

62874519R00061